MYSTERY EXPLORERS™

SEARCHING FOR

GHOSTS AND POLTERGEISTS

rosen publishing's
rosen central®

New York

Billy Breman
and Graham Watkins

Published in 2012 by The Rosen Publishing Group, Inc.
29 East 21st Street, New York, NY 10010

First Edition

Library of Congress Cataloging-in-Publication Data

Breman, Billy.
Searching for ghosts and poltergeists/Billy Breman, Graham Watkins.—1st ed.
    p. cm.—(Mystery explorers)
Includes bibliographical references and index.
ISBN 978-1-4488-4762-4 (library binding)—
ISBN 978-1-4488-4770-9 (pbk.)—
ISBN 978-1-4488-4778-5 (6-pack)
1. Ghosts—Juvenile literature. 2. Poltergeists—Juvenile literature. 3. Parapsychology—Research—Juvenile literature. I. Watkins, Graham, 1944- II. Title.
BF1461.B74 2012
133.1—dc22

2011009791

Manufactured in the United States of America

CPSIA Compliance Information: Batch #S11YA: For further information, contact Rosen Publishing, New York, New York, at 1-800-237-9932.

CONTENTS

INTRODUCTION

Any seasoned campfire or slumber party storyteller knows that ghosts have the power to fascinate and terrify people of all ages. But are they real or just visions captured by an overactive imagination?

Ghosts, hauntings, and poltergeists have been a part of the beliefs of people all over the world since the beginning of recorded history. Ghost stories and movies about haunted houses, even more recent ones like *The Haunting* or *Ghostbusters*, continue to draw in large audiences even in our age of computers and "high tech" marvels. But do people still actually believe in such things as hauntings? Today, you often hear people say, "There's no such thing as a ghost."

In fact, though, there exist places even in the most modern cities where, at times, things happen that defy ordinary scientific explanation. Are ghosts really responsible for mysterious knockings? Do mysterious cold spots mark the sites of murders? Are there truly such things as haunted houses?

There is now a branch of science that studies exactly those phenomena. It is called parapsychology. Scientific parapsychology began in Cambridge, England, in 1882, when the Society for Psychical Research was established. Experimental parapsychology began in the 1930s, when J. B. Rhine established the Department of Parapsychology at Duke University in Durham, North Carolina. This department later became the Institute for Parapsychology. Research subjects for parapsychologists include ghosts, hauntings, and poltergeists.

None of these scientists would say, "There's no such thing as a ghost." For them, a ghost might not be exactly what it has always been thought to be, but sometimes they come upon some truly strange occurrences in old houses and castles thought to be haunted.

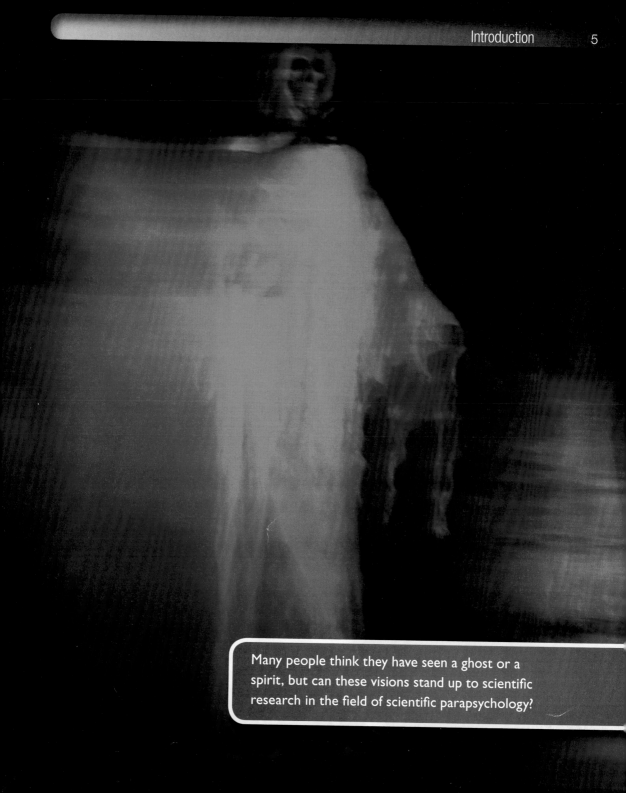

Many people think they have seen a ghost or a spirit, but can these visions stand up to scientific research in the field of scientific parapsychology?

CHAPTER 1
Ghosts and Hauntings

Few people are unfamiliar with ghosts, even if they have never encountered one. A ghost is the spirit of a person who has died; the spirit for some reason remains here on Earth. It may feel it has unfinished business that prevents it from leaving. It may haunt the place where it died or even just a place it felt a very strong connection with during life.

That they are the remaining spirits of departed people is perhaps the most common belief concerning ghosts—not just in our society, but among different cultures around the world across the span of human history. For example, some Native American tribes believed that the spirit of a person who was scalped could not rest unless certain rituals took place. If these rituals weren't completed, or weren't performed correctly, the ghost would remain and be very troublesome to the tribe. In Christian belief, the souls of people who have died are not

Certain Native American groups, like the Hidatsa tribe seen here, had specific rituals they would perform to prevent people who were scalped from becoming ghosts.

expected to remain among the living—and if they do, people question why they have not "gone on" as they were expected to do.

The reasons, as anyone who has ever read a ghost story or seen a movie about ghosts knows, usually have to do either with the way the person died

TYPES OF HAUNTINGS

n many tales, ghosts are associated with specific places we describe as "haunted." Although almost any place, from a building to a car, can be considered haunted, we tend to think first of a house when we hear the word "haunted." The traditional image of a haunted house is usually an old and run-down home in which no one lives.

There are different types of hauntings that parapsychologists have identified. One type is a residual haunting. This means that there is an energy left behind from a traumatic event that happened at the site that is affected. With this type of haunting, people may report hearing footsteps or other strange noises, but they won't feel they can communicate with the presence. A residual haunting is like a video left behind playing over and over again. It is not possible to make contact with a residual haunting. Another type of haunting is an intelligent haunting. An intelligent haunting means that people will feel like there is a ghost present that is capable of communicating with them.

or, sometimes, with events that happened within their lives or the lives of their loved ones. Ghosts are often portrayed as seeking revenge against their murderers. Sometimes ghosts are said to linger on Earth because of unfinished business they must complete. This could range from protecting loved ones or paying for a crime they committed in life. Finally, it sometimes seems that the ghosts have simply claimed a house for their own purposes and are trying to drive intruders away.

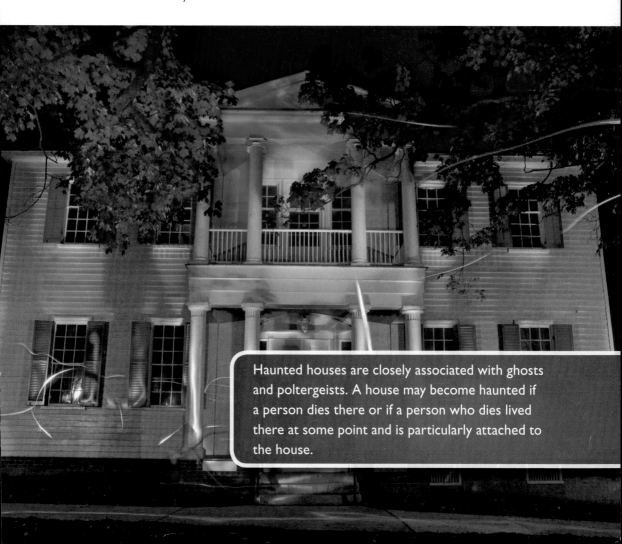

Haunted houses are closely associated with ghosts and poltergeists. A house may become haunted if a person dies there or if a person who dies lived there at some point and is particularly attached to the house.

A haunted house—or any other haunted place—is simply a place where things happen that do not seem to have any natural explanation, at least as far as the people observing those happenings are concerned. The events could range from hearing footsteps when no other people are around to feeling odd sensations like a certain spot in a room feeling inexplicably colder than the areas around it. Some people even report hearing voices or seeing furniture move. Often enough, these strange occurrences are not associated with any known ghost stories. At the moment, no one knows whether a genuine ghost is necessary to cause a haunting, since we do not know, with any certainty, what either ghosts or hauntings really are.

CHAPTER 2

Mischievous Poltergeists

O ne special type of ghost, which produces a special type of haunting, is known as a poltergeist. The word itself is German, meaning "mischievous ghost"—although, as we shall see, poltergeists are probably something very different from ghosts. The most common cases of poltergeist activities involve objects moving about for no apparent reason. Sometimes the objects actually fly around, at times with dangerous force. For example, a glass may suddenly zoom off a table and shatter against a nearby wall.

Although the poltergeist is sometimes considered to be a special kind of ghost, all the evidence we have now suggests that it is really something different.

Unlike ghosts, poltergeists usually infest ordinary homes where ordinary families live. They most often

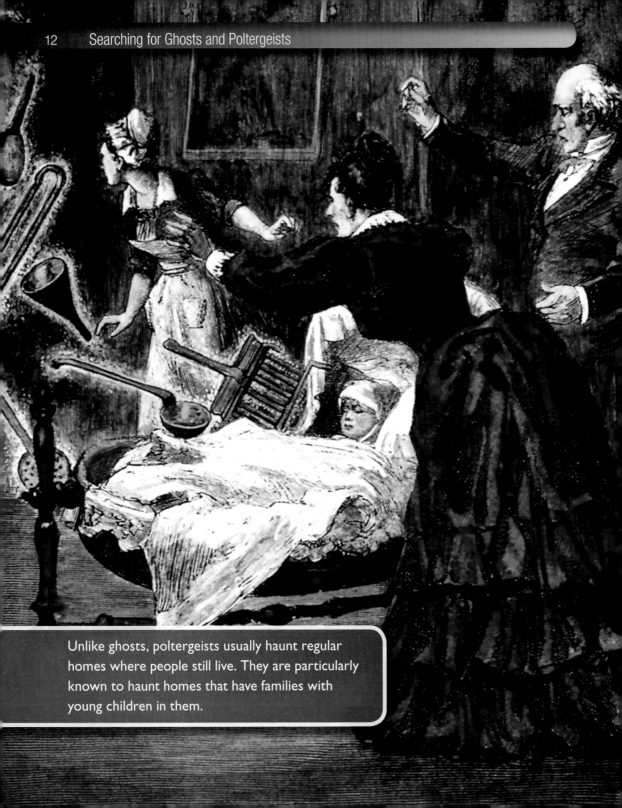

Unlike ghosts, poltergeists usually haunt regular homes where people still live. They are particularly known to haunt homes that have families with young children in them.

appear in families with a child or children near the age of puberty or with children who are overly angry or anxious.

In several cases, investigators have actually observed poltergeist activity in such homes. Dr. William G. Roll, formerly of the Psychical Research Foundation in Durham, North Carolina, has done very extensive studies on poltergeists. Two of his noteworthy studies include the cases of the Callihan family and Robbins family.

Case One: The Callihan Family

In Olive Hill, Kentucky, the Callihan family was being troubled by objects flying about their home, glasses breaking, furniture being overturned, and so on. They left their house for a time in an attempt to escape the poltergeist, but it seemed to follow them.

A researcher directly observed at least two strange incidents. Dr. Roll's associate, John Stump, saw glassware sliding across a counter on one occasion, and on another he saw a chair flip completely over. Later, while in the company of one of the family's five children—twelve-year-old Roger Callihan—Dr. Roll saw a kitchen table suddenly leap into the air, turn partially around, and land on the backs of the chairs that had been placed around it, ending up with all four of its legs off the floor.

Case Two: The Robbins Family

The poltergeist that disturbed the Robbins family in the Bronx, New York, in 1974 was very similar. Pictures would fall from the walls, lamps would fly off

This overturned chair was related to the Enfield poltergeist case investigated by scientists in the 1970s. The activities in that case closely mirror the events that happened to the Robbins family.

tables, and furniture would overturn. In one incident, witnessed by researcher William Eisner, just after eight-year-old Ann Robbins went to bed, a loud crash was heard from her bedroom. When Eisner and the girl's parents went in, they found that Ann's desk and chair had overturned. She was on the far side of the bed undressing. The adults righted the furniture and exited the room.

FIRESTARTERS AND WATER POLTERGEISTS

Parapsychologists have also named some special kinds of poltergeists. One that has been reasonably well identified is known as the firestarter. In cases dealing with a firestarter, objects seem to catch fire for no obvious reason. Another type of poltergeist is called the water poltergeist. A sign of a water poltergeist is pools of water appearing in odd places—again, without any apparent reason.

The special types of poltergeists, such as the firestarter and the water poltergeist, are more rare and have been observed much less frequently by investigators. There has never been a reliable case of anyone who was actually able to start fires at will, like the main character in the book and film *Firestarter*. This type of focused ability remains only in the realm of fiction.

Three minutes later, there was another crash—the desk had overturned again. Eisner noted that the girl's bedroom door was not closed, and his line of sight was such that he would have seen her if she had attempted to dart around the bed and turn over the desk herself.

An interesting aspect of the Bronx case was the way in which objects that had moved once seemed likely to move again. Pictures fell from Mrs. Robbins' wall. She hung them back up, and they fell again. One night she observed a chair leaning back against a wall and put it back on all four legs. The next day, Mr. Robbins and a neighbor found the chair again balancing itself on two legs, the other two suspended in the air. He had to push it back down on the floor.

One reported symptom of a poltergeist haunting is children reporting the feeling of someone watching them sleep. This can be accompanied by feelings of unease and paranoia.

A number of people witnessed the poltergeist activity in the Robbins house, including several neighbors and a policeman who saw Ann's desk chair fall over when no one else was in the room.

Case Three: The Danny Poltergeist Case

Sometimes a poltergeist might seem to follow not a person, but an item. In 1989, Al Cobb purchased a vintage late-1800s bed as a gift for his fourteen-year-old son, Jason. Three nights later, Jason told his parents that he felt as if someone was watching him sleep. The next night, Jason noticed the photo of his deceased grandparents on his nightstand was flipped down. He righted it, but the picture flipped itself facedown again.

Furniture and toys also began moving around Jason's room. Jason and Al later claimed they started receiving notes from the poltergeist after they left paper and a crayon in the room. The notes were in a child's handwriting and were signed "Danny."

A parapsychologist, Andrew Nichols, investigated the case. He told the Cobb family that he thought the bed was just a coincidence and that the events would have happened regardless. He sited a strong electromagnetic energy coming from the wall that Jason was sleeping near. When the bed was put against the wall, that caused the strange feelings of uneasiness that Jason experienced.

But who was writing the notes? It is hard to say because no one ever saw the notes being written. It could have been Jason himself writing them. Mr.

Nichols believed that it is possible that Jason had some sort of psychic ability that was charged by the electromagnetic field he slept near. There is no way to know for sure who is right.

In some cases, as in the Callihan case in Olive Hill, Kentucky, poltergeists seemed to "follow" a family if they try to move away to escape the disturbances. This happened in a case in Bedford, Massachusetts, when the family being tormented by a poltergeist went to a motel, only to have the activity start there, too.

Also, the activity may linger in the house once the original family is gone, as if it were a haunting. The researcher Nandor Fodor has reported a case revolving around a fourteen-year-old girl in which the poltergeist activity continued in the house where the girl had lived, even after another family had moved in.

Chapter 3

Real Cases of Haunted Homes

Haunted houses—or, more properly, haunted places—exist all over the world. In almost every town, there is a place that local residents consider haunted. Some of these haunted houses aren't haunted at all. They are merely old places that have a spooky look about them or have some local legend attached to them.

In many other cases—and these cases account for a large number of so-called hauntings—odd things do happen. However, after careful investigation of each case, many, and sometimes all, of these events that are blamed on ghosts are found not to be odd at all.

Case One: The Fiery Furnace

The renters of an old house in eastern Tennessee were convinced that it was haunted. Practically

At a house in Tennessee that seemed to be haunted, one of the occupants found that his furnace would flare up with flames when he opened it, even if it felt cold to the touch from the outside.

everyone who entered said that it "looked strange" or that they "felt strange," although no one could explain why. The house's occupants complained of doors opening when they had been closed tightly and of objects such as chairs moving on their own. In one case, as reported by the renters, this resulted in a wooden chair dramatically falling down a flight of stairs when no one was upstairs—an event taken by them as proof the house was indeed haunted. One man swore he had been "attacked" by the furnace, an old-style coal-burning heater. He said he had gone to put fresh coal in it when the fire had gone out, only to have flames roar out at him as soon he opened the door.

The mystery of this aggressive furnace was the easiest one to solve—the air ducts had not been cleaned and were blocked with cinders. Although the fire had gone out and the outside of the furnace was cold to the touch, heat remained down in the bed of coals. The fire had stopped burning because it was no longer exposed to oxygen—fires can't burn without oxygen. When the man opened the door, fresh air rushed in. Naturally, the fire roared back to life.

The other mysteries concerning this house were a little more difficult to solve, but some measurements with a protractor gave the answer. The walls were not quite at right angles—90 degrees—to the floors and ceilings. They were, however, very close to 90 degrees. The one farthest off was at 92 degrees. These small differences are very difficult for the human eye to catch. They just look somehow wrong. It is well known that a building with angles just off 90 degrees makes a person feel odd. A number of "mystery houses" promoted as tourist attractions take advantage of this effect.

This slight wrongness was also what was causing the doors to open. The doorframes were not truly squared, and, as a result, the doors, when closed, were under stress, causing them to pop open without warning. The moving objects the renters had mentioned were probably caused by the fact that none of the floors were level and items, including that dramatically falling chair, were simply sliding downhill.

Case Two: It's Raining Seashells

If a certain house in eastern North Carolina was haunted, it was a very unusual type of haunting. According to both the woman who lived there and her neighbors who both witnessed the strange happenings, the house was haunted not by a ghost—but by seashells.

The woman said that, at times, seashells fell from the sky like rain. Sometimes they even fell inside the house. Investigators found that her yard and her roof were literally covered with seashells. The rain gutters were filled with them. Even stranger, the seashells apparently fell only on her property. Neighboring yards showed only a few, which might have been kicked there or moved there by water from ordinary rainstorms. The shells themselves were quite ordinary as well. They were sun-bleached clam and cockle shells, which can be collected by the truckload along the North Carolina beach, which was some 80 miles (129 kilometers) away from the woman's home.

Since the investigators never saw any shells fall on or around the house, this case rests only on the testimony of the woman and her neighbors. Of

Charles Fort, seen here, is known for cataloging hundreds of mysterious incidents of animals or objects falling from the sky. These events are now called Fortean phenomena in his honor.

course, it could have been faked—though why anyone would go to the trouble to truck in tons of seashells and dump them on and around this woman's house remains a mystery.

"Rains" of various sorts of things—fish and frogs are most common—are called Fortean phenomena, after researcher Charles Fort, who recorded and catalogued thousands of such occurrences. We know today that rains of fish, frogs, and similar items are sometimes caused by tornadoes, which occasionally suck up whole ponds and their contents and drop them some other place when the tornado disappears.

Why tornadoes would drop shells on this woman's property and her property alone, and not in the neighbors' yards, would be very difficult to explain.

And then there are some houses—not very many, but a few—that are almost impossible to explain.

Case Three: Ghosts in Amityville

One of the most famous haunted houses is a two-story house in Amityville, New York. The house is the subject of many books and movies. It has become one of the most well-known ghost stories in America.

Part of what we know about the house in Amityville is fact. A real crime was committed there in 1974. A man named Ronald Defeo Jr. killed his whole family one night. When he was arrested for the crimes, he told the police that voices told him to do it.

In December 1975, a new family, the Lutzes, moved into the home. George and Kathy Lutz moved in with their three children and their dog.

Soon after they moved in, strange things started to happen. They smelled odd odors and heard footsteps and knocking at night.

Many strange events centered on one of the upstairs bedrooms. It was often filled with flies for no apparent reason. A black liquid sometimes oozed from the keyholes and vents. The Lutz family called in a paranormal investigator to figure out what was going on. The investigator said he felt very uncomfortable in the upstairs bedroom.

The situation became worse, but no one could figure out why. George was often sick, and the children couldn't stop fighting. One of the Lutzes' children said she had been talking to a little girl in the house named Jodie. The

This unassuming house in Amityville, New York, became famous when the Lutz family, who lived there for only a month, reported experiencing very strange events happening there.

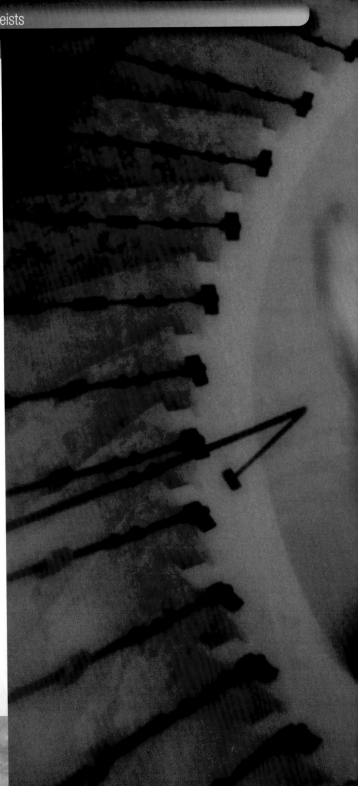

events they went through at the house in Amityville caused the Lutzes to move out after only a month.

Many people have debated whether the events suffered by the Lutzes really occurred. Many families have lived in the house since the Lutzes and none of them experienced what the Lutzes experienced. The house in Amityville went back on the market in May 2010. It is open to anyone with $1.5 million who is brave enough to live there.

Case Four: A Haunting in Kentucky

It is simply called "The Kentucky House" in the

One feature of the reportedly haunted "Kentucky House" was a long, curved stairway. There are tales of people who tried to spend the night in the house being found dead from falling down the stairs.

records because the owners of the property were very reluctant to have the house publicly known as haunted.

An investigation of the Kentucky House took place in January 1970. The house had not been occupied for approximately eighty years. It was a large house of a style associated with the plantation homes of the pre-Civil War South. When it was abandoned, practically all of the furnishings and other household items were left in it. When it was investigated, the rooms were all still furnished, down to the dishes in the kitchen and the books on the shelves in the library. In eighty years, these things had only occasionally been disturbed, so they all remained as they were—except for being covered with a truly amazing layer of dust.

In legend and tradition, the haunting of the Kentucky House began when the young couple for whom it was built spent their wedding night there. They had, so it is said, a terrible fight. What the fight was about no one knows, since neither of them survived that night. According to the legend and to some reports in some old newspapers, the argument ended in tragedy—the young man murdered his bride for some unknown reason, and then, overcome with remorse, committed suicide. The story holds that the young woman was murdered in an upstairs bedroom and that her husband committed suicide in the kitchen. There has not been independent verification of this, however.

There were also stories about how people had tried to spend nights in this house over the decades, and how some of them had died there. Few of these tales are verifiable, but it was said that the causes of death were only two—heart attacks and injuries sustained from falling down the curving

HAUNTINGS THROUGH HISTORY

It's not always possible to say whether anything unusual has happened in a supposedly haunted house or not. The residents—and sometimes the local officials, such as policemen and priests—may tell spectacular stories about ghosts and strange happenings. But researchers, when they visit, see nothing. Many apparent hauntings fall into this category: houses or places where weird or supernatural things are said to have happened, but that offer nothing that can be documented scientifically.

Some of these incidents occurred in places that might be expected to be haunted. For example, there have been dozens of reports of ghosts inhabiting the famous Tower of London, where hundreds of people were killed or executed over the centuries. Some of these ghosts are said to be those of famous people. Many visitors to the Tower have reported sightings of the ghosts of Anne Boleyn, Lady Jane Grey, and Mary, Queen of Scots. Sometimes ghosts are not seen or imagined, but local people tell stories of odd noises or changes in temperature.

At other times the ghosts are apparitions of a very different sort. Abbey House in Cambridge, England, is said to be haunted by two ghosts. One appears to be a nun, but the other seems to be an animal, a strange creature described as looking like a large rabbit but having short ears, and which runs about on two legs like a person. At least two families who occupied this house at different times have reported seeing this odd animal running about the house. What is it? No one knows.

staircases that led from each side of the front room on the first floor up to the second floor.

One of the best-known oddities associated with the house was a "cold spot" located in one of the upstairs bedrooms. This reportedly was the scene of the murder. The cold spot, an area about 3 feet (1 meter) in diameter located near the center of the room, actually did feel much cooler than the rest of the room, but measurements with thermometers showed no difference in temperature between this area and the warm areas around it. Measurements of relative humidity showed no differences either, and there were no drafts to account for the feeling of cold in this spot.

In science, subjective feelings, or the gut reactions of an investigator, are not good enough. Instead, some sort of objective, outside measure is needed. It was decided in this case to bring animals into the cold spot to see if they would react. But the tests were not conclusive. Lab rats showed no reaction. But lab rats have lost much of their natural instincts and thus do not even recognize predators like snakes as dangerous. However, when a cat was brought into the house, she went into a panic from the moment she entered until she was removed.

The next animal that was brought into the house was a rattlesnake. It was hoped that the snake, being cold-blooded, might become lethargic when exposed to the cold, which would demonstrate that it, too, felt the cold, and try to move toward the warmer area outside the cold spot.

Instead, the snake immediately drew itself into a defensive coil and began to rattle. This in itself was very unusual, since this snake had been in captivity for many years and did not rattle at people outside its cage. Even more surprising was that it moved its head from side to side as if following something unseen outside the cage. At least twice it drew its head back sharply, as a frightened snake does when an enemy approaches it closely. Since this was objective evidence of something unusual taking place in the house, the investigation continued. An investigator decided to spend the night in the house.

By day, there was nothing unusual, other than the cold spot, to be seen, heard, or felt in this house. After dark, though, the house became very noisy. Most of the noises sounded like footsteps or like someone banging a fist against walls or, more commonly and more dramatically, against doors. These sounds seemed to come from all over the house.

On the first evening, there was no sense that anything that might be producing the noises was interested in or even aware of the investigator, who stayed in the library most of the night. A book pushed out from the shelf, stopping just short of dropping onto the floor. The investigator, after making some notes, pushed it back into place—and it promptly slid out again, almost as if there was a spring behind it. The book was removed, and there was nothing behind it, but when it was replaced it again slid out—though not quite so far. Over the next thirty to forty-five minutes, the investigator pushed it back into place repeatedly, and, although it kept sliding out again, it moved a shorter distance each time until the effect finally disappeared.

The researcher kept a tape recorder running continuously throughout the night, and, as close to the hour as possible, spoke time markers into the microphone: "It is now eleven o'clock," "It is now one-oh-six AM" At times, the noises in the house were so loud that the investigator wondered if his time markers would be audible.

But later, when the tape was reviewed, it was found that while the time markers were there loud and clear, most of the noises from the house could not be heard at all. Only a few sounds were recorded, and these were usually scraping sounds like that of furniture being moved. In a few places, tracks in the dust suggested that furniture had moved, but no furniture was ever actually seen in motion. In other words, whatever most of those sounds were, they did not affect the tape recorder's microphone—just as the coldness of the spot in the bedroom did not affect a thermometer.

What this suggests is that these noises were not sounds at all, at least not in terms of the definition of a sound as a vibration of the air. The investigator seemed to be hearing them—certainly he would have sworn in any courtroom that he had heard them—but the evidence of the tape recorder suggests that he did not.

Late in the evening of the second night in the house, the investigator, who was again in the library, was startled by one of the loud bangs that sounded like someone hitting a door with a fist. However, this time, the blow was delivered against one of the library doors. At that point, just for an instant, the investigator lost his scientific objectivity as an observer and was at least a little frightened.

Then things changed dramatically. For a moment, the house went completely silent. Then suddenly, all the sounds started again—the bangings, the footsteps, low moaning sounds, noises like distant voices saying words that could not be understood. But instead of being scattered at random around the house, all the noises seemed to be concentrated around the library. It was as if the house had become aware of the investigator's presence for the first time.

The investigator, feeling that he might now be in some real danger, decided to call off the observation and leave. As he made his way down the hallway toward the stairs, the sounds seemed to follow him, echoing out of the mostly closed rooms he was passing. At the top of the stairs, the investigator suddenly remembered all the stories about people who had died from falls here, and, despite being in a hurry, forced himself to hold the banister tightly as he began to descend.

This proved to be an excellent decision. Two or three steps down from the top, the investigator's foot caught on something that felt like a wire or thin rope stretched across the stairs. If he had not been holding the banister, he would have been sent hurtling headfirst down the steps. There was nothing visible on the stair, however.

Now in more of a hurry than ever to get out of the house, the investigator went down the stairs as quickly as possible. He had just reached the front door and was opening it when he felt a hand grab at the back of his neck. The fingers slipped off, as if whatever had grabbed at him had almost gotten him but just missed.

The investigator didn't bother to look back to see what was there. He hurried outside and did not return for his equipment until noon the following day. At that point, he decided to wait for a few weeks or months before trying to stay in the house at night again.

Before any further experiments could be done, however, the owners of the property had the house demolished. There has never been any evidence that the site where it once stood is now in any sense haunted.

CHAPTER 4

The Science Behind the Scares

So far, we have not yet considered what answers the investigators can give us for these phenomena. Unfortunately, there are not as many answers as we'd like, and even now all we can do is speculate.

In the discussion of the investigation of the Kentucky House in chapter 3, it was mentioned that instruments like thermometers could not be used to measure things like the cold spot in the bedroom, and that the noises the investigator heard did not show up on the tape recording.

This type of phenomenon is not unusual. Remember the role that a magnetic field played in the case of the Danny poltergeist case in chapter 2? Studies show that people believe they can see strong magnetic fields, usually as a purple glow, and continue seeing it even if a solid wall is placed between the magnetic field and the viewer. But a camera does not record any glow. In fact, the person is

Paranormal investigators use complex equipment to try to gather evidence at sites that are reported as haunted. This equipment often includes devices to measure the strength of nearby magnetic fields that might cause people to feel strange sensations.

not seeing the magnetic field at all. He or she feels the field—which is strong enough to move the iron in blood—but has no natural point of reference for the sensation, since magnetic fields this powerful rarely occur outside a laboratory. So he or she interprets the unfamiliar sensation as "seeing," rather than "feeling."

In the early 1970s, a series of experiments was performed at the Institute for Parapsychology in Durham to test for a psychic healing ability in some people. The results were published in the *Journal of Parapsychology* and in *Research in Parapsychology*. In these studies, pairs of white lab mice were anesthetized with ether. The task of the human subject was to wake up one of the mice faster than its companion (called the control mouse)

FEAR CAGES

It is possible that some of the sounds in so-called haunted houses are a false sensation caused by magnetic fields. The person "hearing" the sounds is feeling something for which his or her brain has no point of reference, and therefore he or she interprets those feelings as noises, or in other cases, as cold spots. The same sort of phenomenon may account for cases where ghosts are "seen" but cannot be photographed.

Investigators of paranormal activity sometimes call areas where there is an unusually high electromagnetic field reading a "fear cage." This is especially true of a closed-in space like a closet or basement that can make a person feel trapped or uneasy. The combination of the small space and the electromagnetic field levels can make a person feel anxiety, paranoia, or uncontrollable fear. As explained above, this anxiety and unease can cause people to report a haunting because they can't explain the strange feelings they are getting.

could awaken naturally. These studies were highly successful. The subjects were indeed able to awaken their mice much faster than the control mice awoke on their own.

To add to the fairness of the experiments, the experimenters who were handling the mice didn't know which of the two mice they were watching was being "worked on" by the human subject. The two mice were in small plastic pans on either side of a divider on a wooden table, and the human subject was on the other side of a one-way glass. Each experiment was divided into

Paranormal investigators describe closed-in spaces, like basements, with high electromagnetic field readings as "fear cages." These spaces can cause people to feel uneasy and paranoid without knowing why.

two parts, and at the break, the human subject would change sides so that any outside effect—such as drafts—would be canceled out.

The experimenters noticed early on that the human subjects did not do very well with the trials that took place right after they had changed sides. A series of experiments were then done in which the subjects concentrated on one side and then left the laboratory after the break, while the experimenters continued to put etherized mice on the table as if the human subject was still there.

The results were most interesting. The mice on the side that had been "worked on" by the human subject continued to wake up faster than the controls—as if whatever energy was being used to wake them up was lingering in some way. Even more interesting was that the patterns of the way the first half had gone persisted into the second half, when there was no subject. In other words, if the subject had been waking up his or her mice very fast at first and then less dramatically toward the end of the half, the second half would follow in the same way. A large number of these studies were performed, and the results were so dramatic that the odds of this happening by chance were one in billions.

This means that not only did some sort of energy linger, but in some way, information about what had happened in the first half of the trial lingered into the second half of the trial. During these studies, it was found that the effects lingered for about thirty minutes—just about the same amount of time during which the book persisted in pushing itself out from the shelf in the Kentucky House.

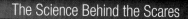

A 1970s experiment used white lab mice anesthetized with ether to test how well people who reported having psychic healing abilities could affect the speed at which the mice woke up.

Two other findings from the mouse-ether series of experiments are important to our discussion. It was found that the human subjects showed elevated heart rates and lowered skin resistance, a response that scientists call general adaptation syndrome, which is the state your body goes into when you are angry, frightened, or excited. Subjects who couldn't wake the mice were found not to be in this state. When they were trained to go into that state by using biofeedback, they were able to perform almost as well as the naturally successful subjects.

The other discovery was just as interesting. The wooden table being used had a metal supporting plate. Grounding this plate—simply attaching a wire from the plate to a nearby water pipe—completely stopped the human subjects, even those who had been successful before, from having any effect on the mice.

Wood does not conduct electricity. A metal plate like the one under the table does, and so does the body of an animal or a person. When you put two pieces of conducting material on either side of an insulator (a material that does not conduct electricity), you have made a capacitor, a device that can store electrical energy. However, if one of those conductors is grounded, the energy can drain away.

These studies seem to indicate that the force used to wake the mice behaves in the same way that electrical energy does. This force, however, is not simple electrical energy, since it cannot be detected by the use of an electroscope.

So how does this apply to hauntings and ghosts? If the stories about the wedding night murder in the Kentucky House are true, then the people involved were certainly feeling the effects of the general adaptation syndrome at the time of the tragedy—great anger for one, and great fear for the other. This could have led to a release of huge amounts of the same sort of energy that was being used to wake up the mice.

That the house was old—more than one hundred years old at the time it was demolished—means that it was originally built without plumbing or electrical service. In many of these old houses, plumbing and wiring were added later; pipes do not run under the houses much, and the wiring is ungrounded. A modern house, by contrast, has electrical grounding all though and under it—and this might well explain why haunted houses tend to be old structures. In the newer ones, the energy does not remain because there are electrical grounds to drain it away. The fact that this force seems to be "programmable" in some way—as we have seen in the mouse-ether experiments—means that these old structures could retain patterns related to whatever caused the haunting in the first place for a very long time.

Another possibility—and this is just as likely—is that the energy does not carry a "pattern" of this sort, but may be in some way directed by the people living in the house. This means that if they are frightened, the energy might show itself as threatening—in other words, giving them what they expect. The fact that the Kentucky House did not seem to "notice" the investigator until he was frightened makes this a real possibility.

Some current research makes this second theory of hauntings seem even more likely. Dr. Roll, mentioned earlier, discovered that a number of haunted houses seem to show electrical or magnetic disturbances. These may have been caused by the haunting or they may have come before it, making it

It's possible that the state of mind of the people in a haunted house might affect the energy of the haunting. If the people are frightened, then the energy in the house may appear threatening.

possible for that particular structure to become haunted in the first place. As yet, we do not know enough to be sure which.

Poltergeists, based on the research that has been done on them, do indeed seem to be very different. You may have noticed in the cases mentioned in chapter 2 that each one involved a family with children who were just reaching or had just passed puberty. In fact, this is the most common feature of poltergeist activities—they seem to always center on a child. In several of the cases, the children involved have been examined by child psychologists and have been found to have some psychological problems—they are usually overly angry or anxious. The theory that scientists have put forward is that these troubled children, with all their pent-up emotions, are causing the poltergeist activity themselves, through psychokinesis—the movement of objects by the force of the mind alone. That is why poltergeist activity is referred to in scientific literature as RSPK, or recurrent spontaneous psychokinesis.

These abilities are not under the child's control. In fact, the child in question normally does not even know that he or she is causing the activity. This, of course, is why the activity often follows a family when they move out of a house to escape the disturbances—since they take their children with them, they are taking the cause with them as well. Those cases where the activity remains in the house, as mentioned in chapter 3, may be explained in terms of the "linger effect" discussed above.

Of course, there are a few "poltergeist cases" where a child has been caught creating the disturbances by ordinary physical means, such as magnets or strings rigged to pull things over. These "cases" have a separate name: fake!

CHAPTER 5

Spirits Take Hollywood

Going back to the early plays of Shakespeare, ghosts make powerful appearances in storytelling. Ghosts have haunted their way into our imaginations through popular culture. Haunted houses make the perfect setting for a spine-tingling scary movie, and the spirits of long-dead men and women are frequent characters in books and television shows. Ghosts and poltergeists are sometimes portrayed as malevolent spirits, and other times as friendly or even funny creatures.

Ghosts on the Silver Screen

Ghosts and poltergeists can make a movie very scary. Atmospheric horror movies like *The Others* tell the story of what it can be like to live in a haunted house. The characters in the movie, especially

A popular ghost, who is far more funny than scary, is Nearly Headless Nick from the Harry Potter series of books and movies. Other than his gruesome appearance, this ghost seldom inspires chills.

the young children, begin to communicate with other children despite their being none in the house. Their mother starts to wonder: are there ghosts in her home?

Ghosts aren't only seen in traditional horror movies. Sometimes ghosts and spirits are used as more minor characters in other genres of films. An

HUNTING GHOSTS ON TV

Popular shows like *Ghost Hunters* have increased many people's knowledge of paranormal activity and the things that may cause it. *Ghost Hunters* follows the efforts of a group of men and women in an organization known as TAPS (The Atlantic Paranormal Society). The members of TAPS call themselves "paranormal investigators," and they travel the world responding to calls from people about supposedly haunted places.

They record their investigations for the television show. In each case, the investigators take a scientific approach to trying to either prove or debunk the haunting. The investigators use complex audio and visual equipment to back up their personal observations as they spend the night in the locations that have included everything from personal homes to Irish castles.

example is the movie *Pirates of the Caribbean: The Curse of the Black Pearl*. This movie is an action-packed and, at times, comedic story. However, the addition of a troop of ghost pirates adds an element of fear to an otherwise not very scary film.

Jason Haws and Grant Wilson are two founding members of The Atlantic Paranormal Society (TAPS) who film their investigations of paranormal activity for the hit television show *Ghost Hunters*.

However, if not all movies with ghosts in them are horror movies, not all ghosts in movies are even intended to be scary. There are some ghosts, like the much-loved Casper, who are both friendly and loveable.

One ghost who is more grumpy than scary is Nearly Headless Nick from the Harry Potter series of books and movies. This ghost haunts the Hogwarts School of Witchcraft and Wizardry. While he doesn't represent a dangerous presence, he does make for a sometimes unpleasant sight as he walks around with his nearly severed head.

The movie *Beetlejuice* is a comedy that takes a different spin on the classic tale of the haunted house. The movie still focuses on the trouble inflicted by ghosts on the unsuspecting new occupants of a haunted house. However, it does this from the point of view of the ghosts—a young couple who died in a car crash shortly after finishing their dream home. They want the new family that moves into their home out so that they can go back to enjoying living there together. They hilariously begin haunting their home trying to scare away its new occupants.

CHAPTER 6
Conclusions

What can we conclude from all these cases, and from all the research done on ghosts and hauntings? Do we finally know all the secrets about ghosts and hauntings?

No, we most certainly do not. With all the scientific research that has been done, we still don't know exactly what those things we call ghosts and poltergeists are. The research into the causes of hauntings marches on, as scientists continually develop new methods for studying unexplained phenomena. But plenty of questions still remain unanswered, and for now, the ghosts seem to be holding onto their secrets very well. There are simply too many cases where the only evidence is a feeling. People experiencing the feeling of unease, strange sounds, or a cooler temperature without explanation might swear on their life that something paranormal happened to them. However, unless some sort of scientific device—a thermometer, a tape recorder, etc—can record it, there is no proof. What's more, there are several cases that don't fit the theories very well at all. For all anyone can say, the ghost of Anne Boleyn, to take one example, really may still be roaming the corridors of the Tower of London.

What we can say is that ghosts and poltergeists do exist. They aren't necessarily living in our haunted houses or lurking around our antique beds, and if they are, it is always difficult for scientists to prove. However, they exist in our folklore and in our movies. As long as we can turn on a movie like *Ghostbusters* or enjoy some scares along with the TAPS team in an episode of *Ghost Hunters*, then ghosts are a part of our culture—whether they are real or imagined.

But the truly important think to know is what you should do if you should happen to encounter a ghost, and it seems to be threatening you. The best advice we can give you is to find a water pipe and stand over it! You may then "short out" any electrical phenomenon.

If the ghost remains despite that…well, all we can recommend then is that you'll have your very own chance to investigate a secret file!

anesthetize To use drugs to make a person or animal unconscious, often for the purpose of surgery.

capacitor A device that is capable of storing electrical energy. It consists of two conductive plates separated by an insulator.

conductor A device or material that is capable of conducting electricity.

control The part of a scientific experiment to which nothing is done; it is used for comparison with the other part or parts of the experiment.

electromagnetic field The field of force produced by the interaction of electric and magnetic forces and that possesses a definite amount of electromagnetic energy.

electroscope A device consisting of two metal leaves that spread in the presence of an electrical field (because both get the same electrical charge, and like charges repel each other).

ether A colorless liquid used by scientists as an inhalation anesthetic.

fear cage A confined area, such as a closet or basement, with very high electromagnetic field readings.

firestarter A specific type of poltergeist whose presence is recognized by the occurrence of unexplained fires.

Fortean phenomena Odd and unexplained occurrences that do not fit known categories. The term comes from the name of a documenter of such occurrences, Charles Fort.

general adaptation syndrome A series of biological events that occur in the body of a person or animal to ready it for strenuous physical activity.

genre A type of literary or artistic work.

ghost An unexplained apparition usually thought to be the spirit of a deceased person.

ground The charge of the earth itself, used as an electrical reference point.

haunting Unexplained sights, sounds, smells, or other sensations that occur regularly over a period of time in a specific location.

insulator A material that does not conduct electricity.

intelligent haunting A type of haunting in which the people experiencing it feel as if they can communicate with the ghost or spirit.

linger effect In parapsychology, the persistence of a paranormal phenomenon in or on a certain place.

objective evidence Data or indicators that conclusively prove that something exists or is true.

paranormal Not understandable in terms of known scientific laws and phenomena.

parapsychology The scientific study of all paranormal processes, including psychokinesis, ghosts, and so on.

poltergeist A "mischievous ghost" responsible for unexplained noises, movement of objects, and the outbreaks of fires or floods. Poltergeist activity usually centers on a person, rather than a place.

protractor An instrument used to measure angles.

psychokinesis Influencing physical things (moving objects, for example) with the power of the mind alone.

puberty The age at which a child becomes old enough to physically have children of his or her own, usually taking place between the ages of ten and fourteen.

residual haunting A type of haunting that is merely a left-behind energy playing like a recorded loop, unaware of a living person's presence.

RSPK Recurrent spontaneous psychokinesis; the technical term for the poltergeist.

supernatural Something that does not exist in nature and can't be explained by natural laws.

water poltergeist A specific type of poltergeist characterized by causing unexplained pools of water to form.

FOR MORE INFORMATION

Committee for Skeptical Inquiry

P.O. Box 703

Amherst, NY 14226

(716) 636-1425

Web site: http://www.csicop.org

The mission of the Committee for Skeptical Inquiry is to promote scientific
 inquiry, critical investigation, and the use of reason in examining controver-
 sial and extraordinary claims, particularly as related to paranormal activity.

International Parapsychology Research Foundation

1308 Wade Street

Aliquippa, PA 15001

Web site: http://www.iprfinc.com

The International Parapsychology Research Foundation is a diverse nonprofit organization of individuals who, through the application of various
 disciplines of science and academia, strive to deduce logical and relevant
 conclusions to questions in the field of parapsychology that have not been
 adequately answered by conventional or traditional scientific means.

Paranormal Phenomena Research and Investigation

133 Lumsden Crescent

Lower Sackville, NS B4C 2H3

Canada

Web site: http://www.ppri.net

This Canadian nonprofit is a scientific organization that continually works to educate the general public in all areas of parapsychology. One of the services it offers is paranormal investigation of private homes by request.

Paranormal Research Society

P.O. BOX 403

State College, PA 16801

Web site: http://www.paranormalresearchsociety.org

The Paranormal Research Society, more commonly known as PRS, is a professional organization operating out of Penn State University. It is comprised of two research departments: Field Investigation & Research (FIR) and Parapsychology & Laboratory Research (PLR).

Rhine Research Center

Institute for Parapsychology

2471 Campus Walk Avenue, Building 500

Durham, NC 27705

(919) 309-4600

Web site: http://www.rhine.org

The Rhine Research Center is a hub for education and research in the field of parapsychology. The center publishes the *Journal of Parapsychology*, a peer-reviewed scientific periodical that has been published continuously since 1937.

Survival Research Institute of Canada

P.O. Box 8697

Victoria, BC V8W 3S3

Canada

Web site: http://www.islandnet.com/~sric/research_overview.php

The Survival Research Institute of Canada is an organization that pursues and promotes studies in the field of survival research, which is the investigation into whether some part of human consciousness or personality, commonly referred to as "spirit," survives physical death and whether that spirit is able to communicate with living individuals.

Web Sites

Due to the changing nature of Internet links, Rosen Publishing has developed an online list of Web sites related to the subject of this book. This site is updated regularly. Please use this link to access the list:

http://www.rosenlinks.com/me/gho

FOR FURTHER READING

Costain, Meredith. *It's True! Hauntings Happen and Ghosts Get Grumpy.* Vancouver, BC: Annick Press, 2006.

Doak, Robin S. *Investigating Hauntings, Ghosts, and Poltergeists.* Mankato, MN: Capstone Press, 2011.

Gibson, Marley, and Patrick Burns. *The Other Side: A Teen's Guide to Ghost Hunting and the Paranormal.* New York, NY: Graphia, 2009.

Marcovitz, Hal. *Poltergeists* (The Library of Ghosts & Hauntings). San Diego, CA: Referencepoint Press, 2009.

Matthews, Rupert. *Ghosts and Spirits.* London, England: QED Publishing, 2010.

McCormick, Lisa Wade. *Haunted Houses.* Mankato, MN: Blazers, 2009.

Oxlade, Chris. *The Mystery of Haunted Houses.* Mankato, MN: Heinemann-Raintree, 2007.

Shores, Lori. *Ghosts: Truth and Rumors.* Calgary, AB: Edge Books, 2010.

Stone, Adam. *Haunted Houses* (Torque: The Unexplained). Minneapolis, MN: Bellwether Media, 2010.

Teitelbaum, Michael. *Ghosts and Real-Life Ghost Hunters.* Danbury, CT: Children's Press, 2008.

West, David, and Terry Riley. *Ghosts and Poltergeists: Stories of the Supernatural.* New York, NY: Rosen Publishing, 2006.

Williams, Dinah. *Haunted Houses.* New York, NY: Bearport Publishing, 2008.

Zoehfeld, Kathleen Weidner. *Ghost Mysteries: Unraveling the World's Most Mysterious Hauntings.* New York, NY: Aladdin, 2009.

About the Author

Graham Watkins is a trained paranormal researcher who formerly worked at J. B. Rhine's parapsychology laboratory in Durham, North Carolina. Watkins is also a screenwriter and the author of five novels. He is also the author of a number of works of short fiction, and his works are available in six languages. Watkins lives with his wife in Durham.

Photo Credits